news fro[...]

presents
a world première

my arm

written and performed by
TIM CROUCH

with digital material by
CHRISTIAN DORLEY-BROWN

co-directed by
TIM CROUCH, KARL JAMES
HETTIE MACDONALD

my arm
had a private view at the Hayward Gallery in February 2003.
It subsequently previewed at the Zipper Theatre, New York,
and at BAC, London

World premiere at the Traverse Theatre, Edinburgh
on 31 July 2003

BIOGRAPHIES

Tim Crouch *writer, performer, co-director*

Tim is a writer, actor and teacher. He co-founded Public Parts Theatre with his wife, Julia Collins, with whom he worked on eight devised productions, including an adaptation of Ford Madox Ford's *The Good Soldier* which played at the West Yorkshire Playhouse and *The Marvellous Boy* which opened at the Bush Theatre. Recent performance work includes *Endgame* (with HMP Brixton), *The Good Woman of Setzuan* and *Light Shining in Buckinghamshire* all for the National Theatre, where he's an Education Associate. In the USA, *Uncle Vanya, Twelfth Night* and *Taming of the Shrew* for the Franklin Theatre, New York, where he's an Associate Artist. Other performance work includes the title role in *Macbeth* for the Swan Theatre, Worcester, Cardew in Mark Ravenhill's *Handbag* for ATC and a variety of TV and film credits ranging from *Coronation Street* to *Mile High*. *My Arm* is Tim's first finished play. This year he's written *I Caliban* for the Brighton Festival, and *Shopping For Shoes*, for the National Theatre/Art of Regeneration. He's currently developing *An Oak Tree, 1973* for performance in 2004.

Christan Dorley-Brown *digital artist*

Chris Dorley-Brown is a visual artist working with photography, film and audio. Recent projects include: *haverhill2000* (2000-1) in which he photographed and morphed the entire population of a town . Also *torkradio.com* (1998), *livestream* (2000) both co-produced with Zbigniew Jaroc and using webcast technologies. Also with Jaroc, Chris set up the digital educational facility at The Junction in Cambridge, which in the late nineties became a national blueprint for artist-run organisations using hybrid technologies. Other projects include *Potential, Ongoing Archive* (2002), shown at TENT, Rotterdam & The John Hansard Gallery, Southampton and *The Beautiful and the Damned* (2001), National Portrait Gallery.

Karl James *co-director, co-producer*

As an actor, Karl's credits include work with Kenneth Branagh, Declan Donnellan, John Retallack and Tom Stoppard. Plays include *Artist Descending A Staircase* (Duke of York's), *King John* (Bridge Lane), *A Midsummer Night's Dream* and *King Lear* (world tour), plus UK and international tours of *Romeo and Juliet*, *The Tempest* and *Much Ado About Nothing*. As Associate Director at Oxford Stage Company he directed *Hamlet* and the acclaimed *Mirad: A Boy from Bosnia*. He's also directed English and Japanese language versions of *Romeo and Juliet* at the Tokyo Globe as well as productions of *The Idiot*, *Woyzeck* and *The Suicide* in London. After seven years as a founding partner of *tradesecrets*, the UK's foremost arts-based communication consultancy, Karl's latest venture is as co-creator of *The Dialogue Project*, an organisation that promotes and employs dialogue as a stimulus for fresh thinking and as a means of solving important and contemporary problems.

Hettie Macdonald *co-director*

Hettie is a director of film, TV and theatre. Her film and TV work includes *Beautiful Thing* (C4) and *In the Land of Plenty* (BBC2). Opera: *Hey Persephone!* (Almeida/Aldeburgh Festival). Her theatre includes: *Sanctuary* (National Theatre); *The Thickness of Skin*, *Talking in Tongues*, *A Jamaican Airman Forsees his Death*, *William* (Royal Court); *The Storm* (Almeida); *Beautiful Thing* (Bush, Donmar, Duke of York's); *She Stoops to Conquer* (New Kent Opera); *The Madman of the Balconies* (Gate); *The Yiddish Trojan Women* (Soho Theatre); *All My Sons* (Oxford Stage Co); *Three Sisters, Once In a While The Odd Thing Happens, Road, A View From the Bridge, A Dolls House, Who's Afraid of Virginia Woolf, The Slicing Edge, The Nose, The Scarlet Pimpernel* (Ipswich); *Waterland* (Shaw); *A Midsummer Night's Dream* (Chester); *A Pricksong for the New Leviathan* (Old Red Lion); *Shamrocks and Crocodiles* (Liverpool); *Leavetaking* (WPT/Lyric Hammersmith).

news from nowhere

my arm is the first venture for *news from nowhere*,
a company whose aim is to explore the borders
between theatre, education and visual art
through performance, teaching and commissioning

news from nowhere's next project is
An Oak Tree, 1973

news from nowhere
can be contacted at
www.newsfromnowhere.net
07966 184491

We are keen to document responses to any
of the work in this publication. With each
performance of *My Arm*, there will be comments
books available. Also, please feel welcome to
communicate any thoughts to Tim at
simon.martin@newsfromnowhere.net

news from nowhere is supported by

ARTS COUNCIL
ENGLAND

Tim Crouch
My Arm

I Caliban
Shopping for Shoes

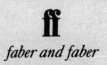

faber and faber

First published in 2003
by Faber and Faber Limited
3 Queen Square London WC1N 3AU
Published in the United States by Faber and Faber Inc.
an affiliate of Farrar, Straus and Giroux LLC, New York

Typeset by Country Setting, Kingsdown, Kent CT14 8ES
Printed in England by Mackays of Chatham plc, Chatham, Kent

A CIP record for this book
is available from the British Library

ISBN 0-571-22193-9

2 4 6 8 10 9 7 5 3 1

To my family

And to the memory of
John, Dorothy and David Wilson

Contents

My Arm 7

I Caliban 39

a story for audiences
ten years old and upwards

Shopping for Shoes 57

a story for audiences
twelve years old and upwards

MY ARM

Thanks

There is a group of extraordinary people who have worked for nothing to get *My Arm* up. At the front of the group, with a Silk Cut and a grin on his lips, is Karl James, who has never been less than inspiring. Also, Chris Dorley-Brown who offered up a fragment of his childhood for this show. Chris' dad, Peter Dorley-Brown, was the man behind the cine camera; his mum, Brenda, gives the show its class. Also, great thanks to Hettie Macdonald for her clarity and encouragement and to Julia Collins for her graphic brilliance, her love, her support, for everything and more. Then the families: Eleanor, Owen and Joe; Jo Cole, Billy and Stanley; Anna Harding, Edwin and Leon. Pam and Colin Crouch, Jilly Griggs, Faye and John Cole.

Plus a few others: Caryl Churchill, Wallace Shawn and John Retallack. Peggy Paterson at Faber. Toby Swift at the BBC. Susan Ferleger Brades and staff at the Hayward. Sam Bond and the brilliant tradesecrets, Jim Leaver, Carolina and Kendal, David Kershaw, Alison Crouch, Virginia Leaver and all who worked with us at the Hayward. Alastair Creamer for Project Catalyst at Lever Faberge. Rick Haythornthwaite at Invensys.

Tom Morris and Louise Blackwell at BAC; Tim Jones at the Arts Depot; Helen Prosser and the National's Young Theatre Company; Gill Foster and City and Islington College (where *My Arm* had its first ever British try-out).

In the US: David Bridel, Ed Vassallo, the Marners and all at the Franklin Stage Company; John Plummer for Owen's arm; Owen's arm; Alan Cumming, Nick Phillippou and Emily Elsener at the Art Party, the inimitable Doyle, Nathan Elsener, Andrew and all at The Zipper.

Introduction

My Arm was written over three weekends in the summer of 2002. The original idea of the boy with his arm in the air came during an improvised story-telling I did for a group of ten-year-olds. In that story were any number of recalcitrant children doing bloody-minded things, but the image of the boy's arm stuck with me. During the same period I ran some workshops for the National Theatre looking at what happens if we substitute actors with everyday, inanimate objects. We performed scenes using fire extinguishers, coffee cups, chairs, whatever was lying around. The objects were manipulated by actors who were instructed not to get emotionally involved with either their object or the scenario in which their object was engaged. This detachment often had the effect of heightening the emotional charge of the scene. It allowed the audience far greater freedom to create their own associations in relation to what was being presented.

So when I started to write *My Arm* the form presented itself very naturally. The boy's action is more meaningful to others that it is to himself. His arm becomes the ultimate inanimate object onto which other people project their own symbols and meanings. The story of the boy whose artless gesture is mythologised ('morphologised') into a cultural icon is mirrored by the audience's investment in the objects they have provided and which are randomly selected to become icons in the story.

My Arm attempts to provoke questions about the qualitative distinctions between viewing theatre and viewing visual art. The visual arts have stolen a march on theatre in their ability to handle progressive forms;

9

the state of modern British art is one of the main engines of the story. While I was developing the play I ran a series of classes looking at the division between the social nature of watching a play and the private, stand-alone nature of looking at a painting. The narrative drive behind *My Arm* is from a clear theatrical tradition; the accompanying visual focus, however, requires a different frame of approach. As an actor, I've often worked far too hard to 'host' an audience's journey through a play; something visual art rarely does. Visual art expects its viewers to work hard. *My Arm* attempts to let the audience be by itself for periods of time, and for me as the actor to feel all right about that. In the previews of the show, some audience members have felt mildly affronted that I haven't taken greater care of them. This is not rudeness on my part, but more an attempt give the audience a greater sense of its own authority in relation to what it is seeing.

Through all this intellectual justification it is easy to forget the fact that *My Arm* is just a story. And as 'just a story', it is able to contain several universes, many of which are personal to me. It has been an endless fascination this last year to trace why only I could have written this like this and what it all means.

*

My Arm had its first reading with the Franklin Stage Company, New York, in September 2002. Last autumn I started to work with Chris Dorley-Brown, the two of us raiding his family's extensive stock of 8 mm home cine footage and talking about the Isle of Wight in the 1960s and 70s. Also, Karl James read the script and has been with it, unswervingly, ever since. We presented a private view of the play at the Hayward Gallery in February 2003. The process from then to now has been one of discussion, minor revision and the occasional preview – in private homes, courtyards, offices, as well as two nights in a theatre in New York City. We have never rehearsed the play in any traditional sense. Later this month Hettie Macdonald is joining us for three days at BAC to try and pin down some answers to a few of the questions we've been asking. The previews at BAC will differ each night as we play with the tone and architecture of the show. As such, the script as published here is not definitive; it marks where we've come so far in fixing something that we imagine will never be fixed.

PRODUCTION NOTE

The following is a suggestion for a note to be read by the audience before each performance of *My Arm*:

This performance is partly about giving ordinary things extraordinary significance. What My Arm *needs is a supply of everyday objects from you: the stuff in your pockets, in your bags, your wallets; stuff you carry around; photographs (driver's licences, IDs, travel cards, etc.), lucky charms, key rings, badges, toys. Useful things; things without function. Beautiful things or ugly things. Things no bigger than a shoe.*

Anything you supply will be treated with care and respect. It will be on stage at all times. No conventional magic will be attempted with it – no hammers and handkerchiefs. You will get it back at the end. But the stuff you supply will create a major part of My Arm. *Please be ready with possible things when they're requested. Thanks.*

Tim Crouch, June 2003

A table-top. Onto this is trained a camera. A chair by the table. The feed from the camera is shown on a television which sits at the side of the stage. Elsewhere on the stage, a much larger screen onto which are projected three sequences of film.

Apart from a doll which represents the performer, the objects and pictures are in no way representational. They should be any kind of object chosen at random. Ideally, they are objects and photos offered up from the audience before the start. All these articles are left, visible but unlit, by the side of the table, like actors in the wings.

There is a measured, haphazard quality to how these objects are given aesthetic significance by the events with which they become involved.

Film Sequence No 1, SURFURY, *plays and ends.*

What I'd like to do is just start . . .

   Silence.

. . . and then at some point later go into words. Words are too substantial to describe the beginning of this story. You know it anyway, or at least it's not hard to imagine it. Connecting it in your minds to the intrigue that may have brought you here; connecting it to a sense of morbid fascination perhaps; or some articles you may have read, or a short television documentary they showed here. Or, of course, to the photographs and paintings themselves. But the start of this story seems incidental now. Coincidental to the theme certainly, if not to the narrative.

He presents his doll to the camera.

Perhaps if I just spoke. And you decided for yourselves
when you sensed a beginning had begun. When we got to
the meat, so to speak.

*A drink of water. He populates the screen with
random objects.*

This is me. This is this. These are these. For those of you
familiar with all this you'll know all this anyway. This
is the television remote control. This is the panic button.
This is my oxygen. These are some of my pills. This is the
remains of a Spanish omelette. There are times when I'm
fed through a tube, when I can't find the energy. But
today I felt like a little Spanish omelette and so far I've
kept it down; I shouldn't be surprised if later on today –

He swipes the objects away.

Whispered tight into the doll.

I'm going to hold my breath until I die.

Don't think that this gesture is about belief. It isn't for a
moment about belief, or conviction or integrity. I'd like
to be able to tell you that this all sprung out of some sort
of social protest. That I was incensed by the stories from
Cambodia. Or even that it was an heroic gesture in the
face of an abusing father, or separating parents, or –
I think it was none of these. If anything it was formed
out of the *absence* of belief. I think at some point I was
struck by the realisation that I had nothing to think
about. I was thought-less. I couldn't cause thought. I was
not the effect of thought.

I was watching a lot of TV, eating a lot of processed food.
It was the 1970s. Heaven.

*He makes the doll fall over. He makes sounds as if
the doll is gasping for breath. He makes the doll sit
up again.*

Look at me now and look at me then.

Heavy matter. A home boy. Devoid of sharp edges, lifts or angles. All plump and soft and thoughtless. Suspended. Without gravity. When we jump up, we're not only drawn to the earth but also, in some small way, the earth is drawn to us. Only for me, at ten, gravity was one-way.

The doll jumps, repeatedly.

Here I am watching TV.

The doll.

Here I am at the dinner table.

The doll.

Here I am reading comics.

The doll.

This is the house we lived in.

He draws a rough picture of a house on a notepad and presents it to the camera.

This is my dad's car.

He presents a photo or an object.

This is my mum's car.

He presents a photo or an object.

This is our dog.

He presents a photo of a dog.

At this time my dad –

He presents an object.

– is a salesman for Artificial Fibres. He drives a secondhand beige Mercedes. He is as old as I am now. My mum –

He presents another object.

– is my dad's professional wife. She cooks fondue. She drinks gin and soda. My brother, Anthony

He presents another object.

– is older than me. We're a middle-class family living in the middle of the 1970s in the middle of the Isle of Wight, which is a small island off the south coast of England.

He starts to pant heavily, his doll moving in time to his breath.

This is me. Hyperventilating. It's 1974, and we're having our tea.

The other objects play out the scene, interspersed with panting.

This is my mother.

Mother Leave him. He'll come to his senses. Eat your tea.

This is my father.

Dad Anthony. Anthony. Sit in. Pick it up. Sit in and straighten up.

This is Anthony's hand. He shows his hand to the camera and pumps his fists.

Mother Stop pumping your fists. You'll crack your joints. Gordon. Gordon. He's turning white. Stop him. Dear God, what have we mrm to mrmermer . . .

The doll collapses. Camera closes up on its face until it is out of focus.

I'm not feeble-minded, if that's what you're thinking. I've kept abreast of things; I can have a good guess at the human condition. Considering I came from where I came from, I think I've done quite well. And so the overwhelming question is why? Why end up here, on my side?

During one of my early visits to the psychiatric profession it was suggested to my mother that, just as the physiological act of smiling can engender feelings of happiness, so, perhaps, somewhere in my mind I had decided that performing an action which could, in the half-light, be considered at least intriguing, would engender sensations of intrigue in me.

Or perhaps it's all arbitrary.

My father would say that it all started at the age of four when, through what he insists to have been an act of will, I didn't pass motion for a month. I absorbed enough of my own toxins to kill a horse, or a Shetland pony at any rate. He says that the look of triumph on my little face, as they administered enemas and suppositories, was the same look I displayed on the cover of *Art Monthly* however many years later.

If that was the first display of my 'self-determination', then I was too young to remember the detail of the will behind it. For that moment, we have to go to the Great Silence of 1973.

> *Silence far longer than is bearable. Maybe two or three minutes.*

You'll appreciate how it must have been for all involved.

I don't know what made me such a . . . cunt.

> *Presents mother-object to the camera.*

Mother Daddy's away till Thursday. I'm out till eight. There's cottage pie, Anthony. Gas Mark 6. Twenty minutes. Tinned peas. Here's ten pence for sweets. That's pudding, or there's fruit. Mr Martin's coming round to look at the boiler. Don't bother him. *His* son's in the cadets. *And* he does judo.

I'm being ruthless in the editing of my material. Thirty years into an hour. One year every two minutes. It's Mr

Martin's son, Simon, whose name is on the leaflets, who's sitting at the back now, whose idea this all was, who doesn't do judo any more. Who's looking at his watch.

And to start with, it wasn't just me. Anthony was just as bad, although he denies it now, of course. If anything, he was worse. As the eldest, he led the way and I, like so often then, just followed along behind, undetermined, indeterminate. Anthony kept a piece of gum in his mouth throughout the forty days of Lent. I held a pebble that I'd picked off the beach at Littlehampton in my mouth for a month. Whenever we travelled anywhere in the car Anthony and I would see who could keep their thumbs inside their fists for longest. We would test each other to see how long we could live on tiptoe, how long we could go without weeing, how long we could make our wees last. Anthony discovered that he could turn his eyelids inside out. I would put needles into the skin on my palms. Anthony once had to see a doctor after having worn a rubber band around his finger for a week and a half. And then there were the silences. If we'd turned our attention towards more purposeful pursuits then perhaps none of this would have happened. But then you would never have heard of me. You might have been spending these moments of your life doing something else.

One evening, when I was ten and Anthony fourteen, we had fireworks.

All lights off. A sparkler lit and burns down. Lights up.

My parents had invited the Martins over for the fireworks. It was summer so it must have been late. Their son, Simon (*object*), was with Anthony and me in the gazebo at the bottom of our garden. I remember not being able to get comfortable. Simon was more Anthony's age and they talked easily.

The scene is played out with the doll and objects.

Simon Four.

Anthony No.

Simon Yeah. Four.

Anthony Who?

Simon Lorraine Dodds. Phillippa Pearce. Carol Payne. Vanessa Doyle.

Me Groovy.

Simon Smell that.

And we had to smell his fingers.

Simon Michelle Stevens.

Anthony Me-smell Stevens.

Me Cool.

Anthony Shut up, spastic.

So, the fireworks over, my brother drifting off, my parents settling into another bottle of rosé, I took myself to my room and –

He raises the doll's arm up above its head, where it stays until the end.

And that, really, is the beginning, the middle and the end.

Apart from Anthony, no one noticed for the first day. That night I stood in front of the mirror on the landing. I took myself to bed and put myself lower down on the bed. I think I thought that the day had been an interesting test and would soon be forgotten.

In the morning there was nothing to do. Nothing was planned. The muscles in my shoulder reminded me of what I'd done the day before and I felt a small tremor of excitement about the prospect of doing the same again.

Instead of going down to breakfast I positioned myself against the headboard of my bed with my arm resting up in the crook of the wall. Very quickly I passed through the threshold of any pain and the discomfort became a little hypnotic. I unbuttoned my pyjama top and looked at the shape of my armpit leading down into the folds of my stomach and up into the tapering of my wrist. Eventually my mother came into my room. I told her, as it was the holidays, I was going to spend the day in bed. She was happy to be free of me for the day. In the evening I came down quietly and placed myself on the sofa to watch TV. That night I woke, aware that I had moved up the bed and brought my arm down. I got up and made a simple cuff which I attached to the headboard. I was then able to sleep with my hand resting in the cuff, my shoulder twisting up from the pillow.

The next day my father was home. Still, I think, my mother hadn't really noticed me. When Dad asked what I was doing she looked as curious as him. I said that I had pins and needles and that it was relieved if I held my arm up. On the fourth day the burning in my shoulder was unbearable. I thought that enough was enough and that was that. I felt elated by what I had achieved but when I brought my arm down I was swamped by a feeling of failure. Also, the pain was as bad with the arm down as it was up. I had clearly reached a halfway mark, where I could go either way. I decided to try another day of it. It was nearly the weekend; if I could get to Saturday then that would be a marker.

Friday was complicated by the fact that I had to go to my aunt's. Mum was concerned that my pins and needles should be lasting so long. I told her it was feeling much better and spent most of the day either leaning against walls or watching TV. In the car I rode home with my arm out of the open window and felt like a super hero.

It felt like it would take more effort to live with my hand down now than up.

The following Monday my dad bellowed at me, slapped my face, shook me and took me to the doctor's. Within a month I had been appointed my very own child psychiatrist. I was the boy with the arm.

He writes the words 'Mrs Williams' on a card and places an object next to it. He talks gently to the doll.

Mrs Williams Is there anything you want to say about what we talked about last week? Do you remember what we talked about last week? Have you thought more about why you're doing what you're doing and how it upsets your mummy and daddy? Your mummy had a cry, didn't she? Why don't you stop it now and make your mummy happy?

Mrs Williams suggested that my action was a plea for attention. She said that everyone feels better about themselves if they feel that they are being noticed, but that in this modern world it was easy to feel invisible. She gave me a small doll to keep, and said that if ever I was lonely or on my own, that I should set the doll up somewhere where it could see me, and then I would feel I was being noticed, and that what I was doing was appreciated by somebody else. This way I would feel that I had less to prove and that maybe one day I would want to put my arm down and get on with things like a normal ten-year-old.

He takes an object and places it some distance from him, where it remains, dimly lit throughout, observing him.

I can't begin to describe my sense of definition and power. I realised for the first time where I ended and the rest of the world began – I felt sharp, delineated. For the first time in my life, the air I breathed had an edge. I was setting the rules. I had a special place in assemblies so as not to confuse visitors. I was excused PE. I spent break time with the school nurse. I was appointed a social worker. People stared at me in the street. No one knew what was going on. They felt threatened. I became the focus of aggression. I triggered insecurities. In 1977, during the Silver Jubilee celebrations, I was approached by two fathers from the school.

The scene is played out with objects.

Man 1 What do you fucking think you're fucking doing?

Man 2 Put your fucking arm down, you fucking twat.

Man 1 Put your fucking arm down or we'll fucking twist it off and stick it down your fucking throat, you fucking freak.

It was the highlight of my life so far.

A slow fight between the doll and the object – acrobatic, presented for the camera.

Because the muscles around my shoulder had started to atrophy, and because the bones around the socket of my arm were starting to skew, and because the ball joint had begun to ossify, when they snapped my arm it tore a blood vessel at the base of my neck.

Fight stops.

And when the doctors set my arm, they had to set it up. And when they took away the cast, the physiotherapist demanded that I work to bring it down. And when I refused to bring it down, my GP referred me to a residential clinic for children with behavioural problems. And my aunt, who attended a spiritualist church in Ryde, declared that I was possessed, and set about arrangements for an exorcism, and my mother resisted her sister's wishes, but determined that we should all go to church so that I could think about things beyond this world. She thought, I suppose, that, as a family, we ought to explore the transcendent.

And throughout this period Anthony (*object*) called me wanker. 'Wanker.'

He said I'd stolen his idea and said that it had gone beyond a joke and that I should fucking stop it. And when I said it wasn't his idea, that in fact, it wasn't any idea at all, he would leap on me and threaten to bind my arm, which is not far off what Mrs Williams finally resorted to recommending as a way of breaking my psychosis.

There was a report in the local paper titled 'Armed Assault: Two Arrested for Assault on Arm Boy.' It explained how I had become something of a curiosity to local residents, and it showed a photograph of my dad. The court case stirred up a lot of atmosphere at home. Looking back on it, I think my mother was undergoing a slow process of grief, although both my parents seemed to be locked in the stage of denial. Life went on as normally as possible. My father became head of a sales division. Everyone in the house either started smoking or started smoking more. Everyone in the house either started drinking or started drinking more. Anthony became one of the few punks on the Isle of Wight, which seemed to upset my mother even more than my irritating gesture. The issue of my arm had been subsumed within the domestic routine. It no longer felt like a questionable act of will, but more like a fact of life, like a squint or a pigeon chest. I had gone past the point of considering a choice in the matter. I had pain, but mostly it felt numb, and the numbness was far outweighed by the continuing sense of euphoria. As well as breathing, smoking, drinking, watching TV and occasionally going to school, this was also something that I did. I adapted my life to my circumstances and felt bemused when people or institutions made a fuss. I did as little with my life as I had done before, but now, when I was doing nothing I had a sense that I was also doing something. This balance kept me held, suspended without future or failure. After a few years, when people realised it really wasn't a stunt, I began to feel my stature grow. Girls began to show an interest, if out of nothing more than a ghoulish fascination. I never mentioned my arm, I lost some weight. In 1979, after Anthony's A Levels, we went to the Balearics for a fortnight. On our return I was referred by Social Services to a residential convalescence home for young people who had undergone trauma. Anthony went to London. To art college in London.

As far as I could tell, the purpose of my stay was for members of the psychiatric departments of several universities to work out what the big idea was. I was subjected to a series of tests, lengthy interrogations about my family, my childhood. I was given the opportunity to confront an imaginary cast list from my life through role play. No one actually asked me to put my arm down, but clearly they wanted a success, whatever that might mean. I was put in a group of similarly aged adolescents with similarly idiosyncratic manifestations. There were twin girls, Helen and Alison, who had refused to open their eyes since they were nine.

Presents photo provided from the audience.

Andy Beglin, who wouldn't open his fists.

Presents another photo.

A girl called Barbara Matthews, who had had the contents of her stomach removed regularly since the age of five because she kept on eating batteries.

Presents another photo.

Myrna Kendall, who refused to wash or cut her nails or clean her teeth, ever.

Photo.

There was an even fatter kid than me who had big issues with his own excrement, so we all kept our distance. And there was Kevin Proctor, who was perfectly sensible but who would never wear any clothes if he could help it.

Presents photo.

Kevin would parade around the corridors displaying the thickest pubic hair and smallest penis I had ever seen on a boy of fourteen. Like a peanut –

Presents a real peanut.

– on a bird's nest.

Presents a real bird's nest.

In all their investigations into the nature of my trauma I remained unruffled. I didn't see what I had to offer them. I got the sense from my parents that they were relieved to have their offspring off their hands. They were busy with their lives, and I don't remember not being busy with mine. Anthony was busy enough with his. He was squatting a house in New Cross with several new friends. Every now and then he would send me a postcard that he'd made himself with details of his new life. One vacation he came home and took a series of photographs of my face. He glued the photos onto a canvas and then painted over them with whitewash. He told me that he'd taken letters that I had written to him, burned them and then displayed the ashes between two plates of glass. He said on the course they were exploring representations of nothingness. This all seemed a little heavy-handed, but I was flattered that he'd felt the need.

At some point, Simon Martin –

Presents object.

– who had failed his exams and had spent a year in Newport taking drugs, went to live with Anthony in his squat. Simon earned money working in a petrol station and spent the rest of his time pretending to be an art student with my brother. Simon, then as now, was distinguished by a ruthless disregard for protocol. Together, he and my brother bulldozed their way through the London scene. Private showings at the ICA, the Serpentine, Waddingtons; New Romantic gatherings in Camden and the West End. Simon operated by the rubric –

He writes laboriously on a placard.

'Art is anything you can get away with.'

This placard remains visible to the audience for the rest of the performance.

Anthony sent me photographs of graffiti they had done on the walls of the National Gallery, descriptions of junk installations they had built in their squat, photographs of women he had slept with. I walled myself up in my bedroom. The psychiatrists had washed their hands of me. The only formal attention I received was from the medical profession, who were concerned that if I continued the way I was that I would start to lose my fingers. Already by the age of sixteen my hand was blackening from lack of blood and most of my fingernails had fallen off. Doctors were worried that the flesh on my arm would become necrotic and, in fairness, on a hot day, the smell was sometimes unavoidable close up. My one concession was to occasionally wear an elasticated mitten, but, by and large, I didn't give it much thought.

Excuse me.

A drink of water.

On December 24th 1982, by a bus stop in Ryde, my mother fell down dead.

Film Sequence No 2, SWIM, *plays and ends.*

I went back to the family home.

At the funeral Dad lost it completely. He was drunk and roared at Anthony and me about how ashamed he was of us, about how unhappy we had made our mother and that we were probably the cause of her death. I left home and went to live with Anthony and Simon and a girl called Carla in a new squat near Hackney Marsh. When I arrived, Simon had got hold of the carcass of a horse from an abattoir and he and Carla were busy stripping the remains of the sinews and bleaching the bones. They had no idea what they were going to do with it, but it had only cost ten quid. In the end the project was ditched, but the house smelt of rotting horse for – well, for as long as we were there, which was nearly five years.

My arrival in London made me aware of just what kind of a figure I cut. My mum had adapted most of my clothes so I could put them on easily and, unconsciously, she had hit the style of the time. I was still overweight, but sunken eyes and pale skin seemed to be the fashion. In Hackney I had a room of my own, a portable black-and-white television and a corner shop, which meant I rarely had to travel far from the house except to sign on and collect my benefit. Anthony provided me with a regular supply of soft drugs, cigarettes, pornographic magazines and fizzy drinks. Heaven. He busied himself welding kinetic sculptures in the garden. He had moved away from being jealous of me and now cast an over-protective net around my movements. I continued much as I had done on the Island.

Here I am watching TV.

The doll.

Here I am eating.

The doll.

Here I am reading pornography.

The doll.

Years passed like this.

For long stretches of time I would draw the curtains, switch off the lights and sit in the darkness.

All lights out. Complete dark.

Lie on my bed. Stroke my arm. Move about. Get comfortable. Feel myself. Move over here. Walk here. Stand here like this. There was an exquisite sense of abdication, listening to life outside the house. Listening to Carla and Anthony talking, doors closing, friends coming by, music. An older woman called Sue took an interest in me. She was thirty-one and overweight like me, an actor who worked for a temping agency. One afternoon in the dark she took her clothes off and lay next to me. We both lay very still. I was wearing a black-and-red-checked mohair sweater. My hair was long; down to here, unwashed. I think Sue thought I would say something important. I held my breath. She became upset and whispered things to me I couldn't hear.

Whispering.

She got dressed and left. I watched a re-run of *Blake's Seven*, relieved that she had gone.

Lights up bright. Too tight focus on his doll.

When I was twenty-two I became officially registered as disabled. Bits of me kept breaking down, and then they were fixed. I was in and out of hospitals with various blood infections. My lung collapsed. I lost weight. At one point a doctor suggested that if I wanted to live a normal life I would have to have the arm amputated. It was as though he was proposing I murder someone. I was over twenty-one, so no one could force me unless I was sectioned. But nobody sectioned me, although people often talked about it. I conceded to having this finger removed because it was dead. My blood pressure was 180 over 130.

A drink of water. Film Sequence No 3, RUN, *plays and stops.*

Anthony's art had moved a long way from representations of nothingness. Tired of welding bits of scrap which nobody wanted, he became involved in a community darkroom and presented a small exhibition of photographs showing the detritus left by the police charge at Orgreave during the miners' strike. Carla flirted with being a performance artist, before moving to Cornwall where she became a teacher. Simon left the house to live in Pimlico with a Slade graduate called Erica. Through Erica, whose father was an art dealer, he got invited to go to Berlin to work as the studio assistant to a very famous German neo-expressionist who liked to put horrible and disturbing things in glass boxes and sell them here for thousands of dollars.

When Simon came back from Berlin he asked me if I would work with him on an exhibition that he was planning. It was called Man-i(n)festation, with a hyphen after the 'Man' and brackets around the 'n' of 'in'.

He writes the title out for the camera.

And it was all about me. I was even in it. I went along with it all out of – out of nothingness really. Simon's idea was – would you like to explain it yourself?

Simon's idea was, I think, that I was a bit of an oddity. He took photographs of me, naked. Naked sitting on my bed. Naked in the bath. Naked by the stump of a tree in Erica's garden. I felt like Kevin Proctor.

Re-presents the peanut.

He photographed me clothed and out and about, signing on, outside a newsagent. By each photograph which was displayed in the exhibition were descriptions of social and military injustices made to look like my medical records. One room contained huge lithographic reproductions of the texture of my arm and hand, with titles such as 'Death in Life'. Another had a smaller collection of double-exposure Polaroids with healthy arms superimposed on images of me sleeping, as though I was dreaming about the arms. The centrepiece of Man-i(n)festation was me, sitting in a cradle for three two-hour shifts each day, watching television through ear phones. Bulgarian chants were piped through the gallery. I should have enjoyed the attention, but didn't feel able. The exhibition was a great success. 'Death in Life' was bought by a Harley Street plastic surgeon for £2,500. Simon gave me £200. A journalist called Chris wrote a piece about Man-i(n)festation which was published in a small art magazine. He praised Simon's 'textural acuity' and recommended Simon's 'nominative effectualism' as a way of 'eliding the dualistic conceits of conception and perception'. Even though the gallery was in Barnet, Simon made sure that everyone who should see Man-i(n)festation saw Man-i(n)festation. He sold some of the Polaroids, a couple of the prints and spent several months trying to interest publishers in producing a book of the exhibition.

Anthony didn't see Man-i(n)festation, but wrote an angry letter to the gallery. He was working for a Refugee Action organisation encouraging refugees to document their experiences through collage. I told him I wanted to move home to the Island.

Not having cried for as long as I could remember, I had now taken to crying like a new-born lamb looking for its mother in the rain.

Dad had married a woman called Barbara –

Photo or object.

– but I was too ill to go to the wedding and Anthony had decided to stay and look after me. A few months later Dad came to London on business and the three of us attempted some kind of reconciliation in a wine bar in Finsbury Park.

Three dolls sit in silence. Moved into different configurations. Silence.

Dad took me home.

Barbara hated me. Hated Anthony. Probably hated Dad. But Dad could now afford to play golf and Barbara loved golf. This was the golden era of daytime, confessional TV and Barbara and I would sit across the lounge from each other, drinking sherry, smoking Dunhills and watching a trail of battered lives parading before us. Barbara's initial tactic towards me was a kind of warped maternalism – suggesting activities, therapies. She even once asked me if I'd like to help her bake a cake. Being in the family home again induced none of the intensity or comfort I'd hoped for. Dad behaved as if I wasn't there. He'd become thick with Mr Martin –

Presents object from the fight.

– which, after the Silver Jubilee incident and the court case, seemed a bit rich. They played golf together and Mr Martin would regale my dad with tales of his own son's success in the London art scene. Simon was now curating a small gallery in Bethnal Green and displaying bits of his own work in a gallery here. This only fuelled my dad's resentment of me. I had become a totem of all that was wrong with the younger generation. And I was nearing thirty.

He lays his doll down.

I tried to kill myself by taking Barbara's car and driving it into a tree. As I couldn't drive, I couldn't get up sufficient speed but a set of golf clubs in the back seat ruptured my spleen and I had to have an operation. You can see the scar.

He lifts his shirt over his head to show.

When I came out of hospital Barbara said it was the last straw. She said I stunk out the house and that I would have to leave. Dad was looking into residential-care homes when Simon Martin phoned.

The scene is played out.

Simon It's Si.

Me Hello.

Simon What are you up to?

Me How's Erica?

Simon Brilliant.

Me Right.

Simon I have a suggestion.

Me Right.

And Simon told me of a famous painter whom Erica had befriended. This famous painter had seen photographs of me and felt she wanted to use me as a subject. I told Simon that I had nowhere to live. He said that he and Erica had bought a flat in St Catherine's Dock, that there was a spare room and that I could come and live with

them if I wanted. I said I didn't know what I wanted.
Simon said he would act as my manager; he would look
after me.

The famous painter's studio was in Notting Hill Gate.
She painted at night; she would need me to sit over a
period of at least nine months as and when; she would
pay me £8,000. She also offered to cover any medical
expenses I incurred during that time and to pay for a taxi
to get me back and forth from Simon's flat. She offered to
show me some of her other paintings, but I said I wasn't
interested. She told me that she liked to paint people
naked and asked if I would mind taking my clothes off.

   He picks up the doll of himself and holds it in front of
   him. This must feel like a break of convention.

Those nine months were the beginning of my life. *This* is
the beginning of the story. Nine months felt right; it was
a gestation, and the finished painting was my rebirth.
On the first night she got me to stand in the middle of her
studio, legs slightly apart and to look just past her. My
hair was shorter than it is now, but we took it out of its
ponytail and it rested on my shoulders. I kept my glasses
on. I can't see without my glasses. And that was it. She
looked at me for half an hour, moving around me, and
then we rested and talked. Then another half an hour and
she made some lines. Then she asked me to look directly
at her, to stand in a similar position but to put slightly
more weight onto one leg. Half an hour looking, half
an hour chatting and then some lines on the paper. She
said she was looking for my composition. At three in
the morning she opened a bottle of wine. We drank it,
she ordered a taxi and I went home. Two days later she
called me and the process continued. We worked under a
bright naked light bulb. There was no refuge or pretence.
She hid nothing of what she was doing from me. She
didn't want me to pose, but just to be. As soon as my

33

concentration wavered, if I thought about other things, then she knew it and we rested. It was a feat of endurance for both of us. I felt illuminated – as though her focus was a searchlight which picked me out. Sometimes she asked me to talk about my life. Sometimes she just did sketches of my arm as I sat on a sofa. Sometimes I wouldn't be called for a week or more as she was working on other paintings. Sometimes I couldn't see her because I was attached to a drip. My blood pressure was 210 over 150.

We worked together on four canvases over four years – plus a sheaf of sketches, line drawings, charcoals.

> *He presents compositions of himself with the doll direct to the audience.*

I felt redeemed. I felt meaningful like somebody other than yourself is meaningful. For the first time ever I wished I could retract everything, go back, counsel myself out of myself on that night with the fireworks. Bereavement and redemption in the same breath.

The paintings won awards. I became renowned. People wanted to meet me. I was too ill to do anything, but I became observed, which perhaps is all that anyone other than yourself can hope to be. There were articles and interviews. Channel Four asked to make a documentary. This is probably where you start to come into the story. Other artists made approaches but Simon took control. He and Erica started to make casts of my arm. Two bronzes were made.

> *He presents objects.*

One is in the Hirshhorn in Washington, the other is on permanent loan to the Musée National d'Art Moderne at the Centre Georges Pompidou in Paris. There are maquettes of my arm in Madrid, London, Birmingham, England and here.

A drink of water.

Anthony was living with a South African girl called Kim in Stoke Newington. He was organising an exhibition of refugee art for a studio in Hammersmith and spent much of his time writing evaluation reports to the Arts Council. Kim was pregnant, but Anthony offered me a room in the house if I wanted it. I said I didn't know.

I suggested to Simon that now would be a good time to stop what had started twenty-five years before. A consultant at Guy's Hospital had suggested that some of my medical ills could be remedied on condition that the arm, much of the shoulder and my left lung were removed. He offered his services and described the operation and what it would leave me with.

He draws a diagram of himself on a notepad, marking a line and scoring through where the arm would be removed.

Simon was resistant, weren't you? He wanted to take me to the States. I couldn't fly because of the danger of thrombosis, but Simon offered to pay for a trip across the Atlantic by boat. Erica's father was friends with the foremost American art dealer, who was interested in meeting me. Simon urged me to consider putting off any operation until after we'd met. He said that this man had single-handedly resurrected the US market in modern art; he owned three galleries in Manhattan, one in Los Angeles and one in Washington; he determined market values; he could make or break an artist's career. Simon was persuasive. The US art world was clamouring to see me, he said. And after all he had done for me, we took a boat trip to New York. Anthony came to wave me goodbye. This boat was nothing like the Wightlink ferry.

Reprise of Film Sequence No 1, SURFURY, *plays and stops.*

We arrived here in the summer of 2001. When I got off
the boat the heat and humidity hit me and I collapsed.
I was taken to a hospital on the Lower East Side, where
they did tests. I was something of a curio to the doctors
and nurses. An English curio. Over the course of my life,
they said, I had diseased my heart. Diseased it beyond
repair. I was too weak to undergo any surgery. Even
amputation would be locking the stable door after the
horse had long ago bolted. There was nothing to be done.
I was an internal shambles and would probably drop
down dead at any moment. At the most I had a couple
of years. I had rotted. I had composted from the fingers
down. Not surprising really, but odd that one small
empty gesture could have had such an effect, and a shame
when everything now seemed to be so promising.

He presents his doll.

In addition to a one-off fee of $250,000, the dealer
offered to pay all my medical and living expenses until
I died. He would also pay to have most of my body
returned to the Isle of Wight for burial. In return I would
sell him my arm. Of course he wouldn't take it whilst
I was alive, but he would have unrestricted access to my
terminal decay – documentary-makers, photographers,
visual artists. Then, after my death, he would have global
rights to display my arm in an aesthetic context to be
determined between him, Simon and me. Any display
would be accompanied by an exhibition of my life,
including family photographs, cine film, school and
medical reports. Simon would oversee the whole package
for an undisclosed sum. He would market the run up to
my death – television appearances, sponsorship deals,
that sort of thing – and he would manage my estate
afterwards. He also arranged for me to do a series of
talks about my life.

He gets up and removes the 'observing' object from its position.

I spoke to Anthony on the phone.

He places his head down in front of the camera, so that it appears large on the screen.

I said I was sorry that I wouldn't be coming back, but that I'd be more than happy to pay for him to come over. We talked about Mum, about the island. Kim was expecting their second child, so he wouldn't be coming over yet, but he would try to in a year or so. He was painting for himself now – small canvases about his memories. He said he'd send me a portrait he'd done of me as a small boy. In it, he said, I was watching TV, plump and contented. With my arm around him.

I CALIBAN

I Caliban was commissioned by Pippa Smith for the Brighton Festival of 2003. It had its first performance at Downsview School, Brighton on 16 May 2003. Many of the ideas were developed with Year Six students at Tidemill and Grinling Gibbons Primary Schools in Deptford, through the Art of Regeneration/National Theatre Primary Shakespeare Project, co-ordinated by Rose Harrison.

I Caliban was designed by artist Jane Lyster, and much of the staging evolved through discussion with her. The story was presented by the Brighton Festival as being 'Shakespeare in a Suitcase', so everything came out of a wheelie suitcase with a tape machine stitched into the side.

Thanks to Claire Bird and Kenna Worthington at Tidemill; and to Pippa Smith, Alex Epps and Stephen Clark in Brighton.

PROLOGUE

Caliban with a bottle. A stack of books at his side. Music playing from an old tape machine.

As the audience come in, improvisation along the lines of:

Oh. Look at you.

Oh, you're beautiful. You're beautiful. I've never seen such beauty. You are such fine things. You're brave spirits indeed. Brave spirits or gods. Are you gods? Are you a god? No? You must be a god with a jumper like that. I've never seen anything so beautiful. Surely you've dropped from heaven. You, yes, you with the glasses. From heaven, I said.

    Etc., until they're in. Music off.

I know what you're thinking. I know. You're thinking what an ugly man. What a bald ugly man. Why have we come in here to see such an ugly, ugly man. What an ugly tortoise of a man. You're thinking, he's not a man. He's more fish than man. A strange fish. Legged like a man and his fins like arms, but a fish all the same. Aren't you? You're not? You should be. I'm ugly. I'm disgusting. Here, look. See.

    Rubber bands totally distort the face.

Ugly enough for you? Could I make myself any plainer? Am I ugly now? Now? Am I?

    'Yes' from the audience.

Well, YOU'D BE UGLY IF YOU'D HAD A LIFE LIKE MINE.

He takes off the rubber bands, picks up a book and throws it out over the audience.

This is my island.

Or, rather, this island's mine.

It's a bit of a mess. But there was a storm. A bit of a tempest, really. The day before yesterday. And of course everything got a bit shaken up. You must have seen that before. When there's a storm? And everything gets shaken up? Things get thrown up. Not 'thrown up', obviously, but thrown up. Onto the beach. All sorts of things in here (*the suitcase*). My mother used to say that it cleared the air, a storm. A really good storm, she said, like a really good poo. Nothing like it. She spoke her mind, my mother. She wasn't afraid to pick her nose, or scratch when it itched. By Setebos, I LOVED MY MOTHER.

He drinks.

He puts a tape in the machine. Flute refrain from Debussy's 'Syrinx' plays.

He listens.

Have you ever had this? It's called WINE. Have you ever had it? You haven't? O, you should. You have? Good, isn't it? I call it CELESTIAL LIQUOR. Until yesterday, I'd never had it. And now, now I only have one bottle left. I ONLY HAVE ONE BOTTLE LEFT. And that I had to fetch from the bottom of the stinking pool.

Moved by a catch of music. He scratches himself.

Wave comes in, wave goes out. Wave comes in, wave goes out.

Freedom, eh. You spend all your life fighting for it. And when you get it, you don't know what to do with it. High-day blooming freedom.

I'm not making much sense, am I? Perhaps if I started from the beginning. Let me find a tape.

He takes out the Debussy and puts in another tape of sea sounds.

THE STORY

What you have to remember. What you have to remember is that this is an island and that I am a monster.

My name is Caliban. Cacaliban, Caca – liban, 'Ban, 'Ban, Caliban, has a new master, get a new . . . Oh, it all sounds so hollow, now that they've gone.

One day, ONCE UPON A TIME, my mother was thrown into a little boat like this.

The boat, the journey.

Put on a boat like this with me as a tiny scrap. And the boat was pushed off from Africa and when it got here the soldiers wouldn't kill my mother, although many wanted to, and they left us here. Mum and me. She'd done some things right, which is why they wouldn't kill her, and she'd done some things wrong, which is why they kicked her out of Africa in the first place. We've all done wrong things. Haven't we?

My mother. I see her in my mind's eye, sitting there, where you're sitting. Well, actually where you three are sitting. A big woman, my mum. Well, she wasn't a normal woman, really. She was a witch, they said. She grew into a hoop. She could do magic. Her name was Sycorax. Much as your mum's name might be Pauline or Julie or Lulu-belle.

Takes mothers' names from the audience.

45

But she was my mum. MY MUM. Would you like to see a picture of my mum?

He gets a framed photograph of an eye – lovingly.

I'll put her here (*a prominent place*).

The joy about being on an island all by yourself is that you can shout as loudly as you like. MY MUM.

Stops tape of sea sounds.

So there were three of us on this island. Me, my mum and my mum's help, Ariel, who was a blooming useless help. Ariel –

Presents Ariel.

– not even flesh and bones like you and me, but an airy blooming spirit who never did what it was told and would pinch me and called me baldy and fatty and farty and would disappear just as you were about to swat it. Eventually, my mum got angry, quite rightly, and did a spell which put it inside a tree for ever. TO SHUT IT UP.

Puts Ariel in 'a tree'.

So then it was just me and Mum. And then Mum got ill. And then Mum died.

And then it was just me. Just me on the island. Just me. And I wasn't very old. I hadn't even really learnt how to speak. But I knew where the springs were for water and I knew how to catch crabs and dig for pignuts. I managed. I was never very clean, but WHO CARES WHEN YOU'RE THE ONLY LIVING THING YOU EVER SEE. I was the king of the island. For years. Until *he* came along. UNTIL HE CAME ALONG AND SPOILED IT.

Figure of Prospero.

Prospero. The tyrant that I serve. The tyrant that I served. Prospero.

And his daughter, Miranda.

Figure of Miranda.

Prospero and Miranda. Not from Africa like Mum and me. But from Italy. The same kind of rickety boat, though. And the same reason for being here.

A similar little boat as before, but this time on wheels, radio-controlled, driven around the audience with Prospero and Miranda in it.

Prospero.

The one-time Duke of Milan. Like a king, he was. Very brainy. Spending too much time in the library, too much time with his books when he should be duke-ing, upsets his brother, Antonio, who thinks he himself would make a much better Duke. Antonio, assisted by the King of Naples, Alonso, decides to bump his brother off. Deals are done and pacts are signed and one late night he dumps Prospero in this sieve of a boat with his baby daughter, Miranda, and pushes them off to drown at sea. Not so Prosper-ous then, old Prosper-o. Just like me and Mum, really. Only, thanks to an old friend, Gonzalo, who stashes food, drink and books on the sieve, he doesn't drown and ends up here. ON MY ISLAND.

Where I'm all alone.

Wanting my mummy.

He picks up another book and throws it out.

I'm talking ten years ago.

So now there's three of us on the island again. On my island. Him, her and me – plus a blooming spirit stuck in a blooming tree. Only HE HAS BOOKS. And he knows how to read them. And I'm finding it hard enough to pronounce the word 'book', let alone read one. So he takes me under his wing. At first he's like a man in front of a bear – all quiet, and soft and gentle; feeding me and helping me and lulling me, and stroking me and giving me water with berries in it, and teaching me the words for sun and moon and me teaching him about the island. And then he gets the measure of me; then he gets into his stride and starts to treat me like a sullen dog and beats me and orders me and shouts at me and I become his servant even though I WAS THE KING. And because he treats me like a dog I begin to behave like a dog. Well, you would, wouldn't you? And so his daughter's growing big and I'm growing bigger, and her hair smells nice and I think things and want things like any dog worth their salt, and she looks at me with big eyes and her skin is soft and I think how good it would be to have little Calibans and so one thing of mine tries to lead to another but he knows everything, HE KNOWS EVERYTHING, and punishes me for even trying and holes me up in a rock like a kennel and gives me such pains and cramps, which he gives without having to touch me because he's read all these books and he's learnt to do MAGIC.

And one of the first things his magic does is to free the airy blooming spirit out of its tree.

Ariel is freed.

And Ariel becomes his help, his aide, his pet, his favourite, his tricksy blooming spirit. It probably tells him things about my mum, what a witch she was, so he treats me even worse. And I lie awake at night imagining how his head would look WITH AN AXE IN IT.

And then, after the thing with his daughter, after the 'incident with Miranda', after I did seek to violate the honour of his child, I think it becomes clear to Prospero that he's been on my island just a little too long and that he ought to get off.

And that, in a roundabout way, is the reason for the tempest. I mean the storm. I mean the tempest.

Loud, howling storm noise. Noise stops.

So if Prospero's going to leave the island and return to Milan, then he's going to have to sort things out with his wayward brother who tried to kill him and who thinks he's DEAD. And as luck would have it a fair wind is blowing a ship –

A big galleon-type ship, also on wheels, also radio-controlled.

– from Africa to Italy, a route which passes by this island, and on that ship is the whole shooting party: Prospero's evil brother who tried to bump him off, the baddy King of Naples who helped Prospero's brother, his son, his brother, the old friend of Prospero's who put the books in the sieve all those years ago, plus all the crew, plus a couple of drunken fools. All returning from the wedding of Naples' daughter to an African. AN AFRICAN, fancy, imagine, AN AFRICAN LIKE ME perhaps. How times have changed.

And so Prospero takes his magic stick and makes a storm.

The storm noise again.

And the ship splits in two and everyone gets wet – including me –

Water into the audience, also plastic fish thrown, chaos.

– and everyone screams – including me –

Screams from the audience.

– and Naple's son gets washed on to the island on his own over here, and Naples himself, with his brother, the old guy and Prospero's baddy brother get washed up somewhere else over there and the drunken idiots get washed up over there and EVERYONE THINKS EVERYONE ELSE IS DEAD. They also think that this ain't no normal island or that weren't no normal storm because ALL THEIR CLOTHES ARE DRY.

He throws several books.

INTERLUDE OF MAGIC TRICK

Prospero's magic, you see. What do you think of magic? I don't trust it, personally. Well, I've never seen it make anybody happy. Shall I do some for you? Some Prospero magic? Taught to me by the man himself on a quiet afternoon by the beach. Years ago, when we were talking civilly to each other.

He puts on a tape of cheesy, magic-trick music. He does a trick, a really good trick, which involves a plant in the audience – a teacher who's been primed – a trick which blows the audience's mind (for details of trick go to www.newsfromnowhere.net/caliban-trick).

It's a trick. It's a power trip. All his spirits hate him as rootedly as I, but because he's powerful they can't do anything about it. Far harder would be to get people to *like* him. And nobody likes him apart from his daughter, who doesn't know any better. True, nobody likes me. But remember, I'm a monster. Magic. It's only a trick. Tricksy. I hate it. Anyone can do it. You just have to learn. Ask your teacher.

End of Interlude.

THE STORY RESUMES

He stops the music. He throws another book out.

So. Here they all are on my island. And this storm has
been nothing like a good poo. And Prospero has some
idea in his head that will make everyone love him or
something. And this particular day I'm in a particularly
bad mood; I'm at the end of my tether. He taunts me for
fun; he comes to me when I'm eating my dinner (oh, he's
full of himself this day), he calls me freckled whelp, he
fills my bones with aches, racks me with cramps, orders
me to fetch more wood. And I curse him,

All the infections that the sun sucks up, from bogs, fens,
flats on Prosper fall, and make him by inch-meal a
disease!

And then it starts to rain. And then I hear a noise and
I get this (*a disgusting gaberdine*) to hide under. And
I'm tired and now there's a spirit under here with me,
tormenting me. DO NOT TORMENT ME, PRITHEE; I'LL
BRING MY WOOD HOME FASTER. And we shiver together
and I know that at any time the spirit will get me. Only,
it's not a spirit. It's a man, a fine man, a god of a man,
like you or you – not you, though –

To the troublemaker, or the latecomer, or similar.

And you must understand that I have never seen a man
before apart from Prosper. And this man has a friend,
and these men have WINE and these men do not beat
Caliban; they name him for what he is (oh, they are wise).

Liszt's 'Hungarian Rhapsody' – wild and fast.

A very shallow monster.
A very weak monster.
A most poor credulous monster.

A puppy-headed monster.
A most scurvy monster.
An abominable monster.
A ridiculous monster.
A howling monster.
A brave monster.
A most perfidious and drunken monster.

And they make me want to sing and dance.

> *He drinks from the bottle, dances, belches, scratches himself and throws another book. Music continues.*

The two god-men are Trinculo and Stephano, the drunken fools from the ship that split in the storm, and they think they're the only two left alive and in return for me serving them for ever as my lords and masters they agree to KILL PROSPERO, to BITE HIM TO DEATH. But, the thing they must do first is GET HIS BOOKS. Without his books he's nothing, he's just a monster like me. Without his books, when he's asleep, they can knock a nail into his head, I tell them. They can brain him with a log, I tell them. Batter his skull or paunch him with a stake, Or cut his wezand with a knife, I tell them. In return for this favour I will lick their feet and they can 'lick' his daughter. Lick lick lick. Lickety lickety. And then there's freedom, high-day freedom.

> *He sings and dances and howls and spins.*

Farewell, master; farewell, farewell!
No more dams I'll make for fish
Nor fetching in firing
At requiring;
Nor scrape trenchering, nor wash dish:
'Ban, 'Ban, Cacaliban
Has a new master – get a new man.

> *He drains the bottle to the last drop. He stops the tape. Silence.*

Nothing. Nothing. Nothing.

So we go in search of Prospero, in search of Prospero's sleeping skull.

But nothing on this island is as simple as it seems.

And I'm only now beginning to piece it all together, because NOBODY TELLS ME ANYTHING.

Whilst me and my man-gods are hitting the bottle and dreaming about our future kingdom, and sharpening our stakes, Prospero has set his tricksy spirit to work. Of course, thanks to stupid magic, nobody from the shipwreck is dead; they're all alive as you or me. And Prospero's working to a plan. He wants to be Duke of Milan again, he wants to go back newer, improved, strengthened. And what better way than to hitch his daughter to the King of Naples' son, Ferdinand. So, in a hurry, not letting the course of true love take its time, he magics Ferdinand together with Miranda and . . .

> *Acted out between representations of Miranda and Ferdinand.*

Ferdinand Ciao, bella. O, you wonder –

Miranda No wonder, sir, but certainly a maid.

Ferdinand Woof woof.

The only men she's ever seen are me and her old man, so even though Ferdinand looks like a dog's dinner by Italian standards, she thinks he's a thing divine. But she's only *thirteen*. What would she know? But her dad says no hanky-panky until after they're married.

> *He throws a book.*

Meanwhile, I'm at the entrance of Prospero's cave, with my man-gods Stephano and Trinculo. All three of us dripping wet and, to put it frankly, all smelling of HORSE-PISS.

It has not been a good day, and once again I feel that Prosper is getting the better of me and that Ariel has been having fun at our expense. In trying to find 'our victim', we went through toothed briars, sharp furzes, pricking gorse, and thorns, which entered our frail shins . . . and last left us dancing up to the chins in the filthy-mantled pool, where we lost all our wine. And now we're here, ready to do the deed, with bloody thoughts, knives drawn, stakes sharpened . . . a little smellier than we'd planned. When, from nowhere, we see the finest array of clothes strung up on a line. Beautiful garments, like yours, but more colourful, dryer, warmer, finer. And by now I trust nothing, but Stephano and Trinculo have stars in their eyes and start changing and Trinculo's all 'O, worthy Stephano! Look what a wardrobe here is for thee.' And I'm 'Let it alone, it is but trash,' and 'Let it alone, and do the murder first: if he awake . . . he'll fill our skin with pinches.' But they don't listen.

And at that moment I learn something about mankind.

And at that moment I realise I've been had.

And at that moment there is a howling like a howling from the pit of Hell. And spirits, spirits like Rottweilers, baying for our blood, bear down on us and we are driven out and our bodies are racked with dry convulsions and aged cramps. Worse than I have ever known them. And I have known dry convulsions in my time.

Rachmaninov – low, menacing.

And Prospero's laughing loudly as though it's APRIL BLOODY FOOL'S. Laughing on the inside, obviously, because he's a miserable git. And he says, 'At this hour lies at my mercy all mine enemies.' And sure enough there's the three baddies and the old fella, frozen in a charm, and there's Miranda and the King's son Ferdinand blissfully playing chess and letting each other cheat because they love each other so much, and there's me and two drunks legging it around the island with rabid dogs at our heels. And, yes, he must be feeling pretty smug, when he lifts the charms and goes, 'Ta-dum, it's me, back from the grave, get on your knees and apologise and give me back my kingdom,' and 'No, I'm so high and mighty that I won't kill you and, in fact, I'll go so far as to forgive thy rankest fault, and everyone loves me and here's your son, he wasn't dead, and here's my daughter and they're going to be married, and everyone on the ship is safe and let's all go back to Italy and live happily ever after.' And then I'm hounded in with the drunks whom I've mistaken as god-men, and everyone laughs and calls me a fish, and I AM IN SUCH PAIN and I get ever so humble, and my head spins from seeing all these people, and I promise never to do anything bad again and seek for grace, but what's the point of saying anything because everyone gets on the boat which is yare and bravely rigged and OFF THEY GO TO ITALY LEAVING ME HERE.

Music off.

And the worst of it is, the worst of it all is, that Prospero – the tyrant whom I served for years, the tyrant for whom I scraped trenchers and washed dishes – he turns to Ariel and blesses him with his freedom, and he doesn't even spare me a backwards glance. And as I watch the ship sail off I look up and see the tricksy blooming spirit's heart burst with freedom and it scatters into the elements. And off the ship goes.

He loads the radio-controlled galleon with all the characters. The journey.

And I watch it go, until it is a tiny speck on the horizon. And then it is gone; all is gone. And I am left with, all that I am left with is the flotsam and jetsam, the detritus thrown up by the storm, and a pile of books. His books.

He throws a book out to sea.

Because, because he doesn't need them any more. Why,
quite frankly, with his magic, he didn't just magic up
a boat and sail back to Milan years ago and ask for an
appointment and sort it out that way I do not know.
He didn't, though. And now, now he has what he wants,
he doesn't need his books. Before the ship took sail, I saw
him break his magic stick and bury it in the earth; I saw
him take his big book, go to the top of the cliff and fling
it down to the sea. And I'm left with these. These
dangerous little texts that only get in the way.

Throws the final book.

Magic. Far better to do it without. A greater sense of
achievement, I imagine. Don't you? Less of a sense of
having cheated.

And so I think, I think I'm better off. I'm better off here,
being this ugly fish-tortoise of a monster. And it's just as
well the bottle's empty; and it's just as well I can't read
magic books; and it's just as well they've gone. I know
I haven't been perfect, I was a thrice-doodle ass to take
those drunkards for gods, but I've been what I've been.
Been what my mother made me, and you can't say fairer
than that.

He picks up the photograph of his mum.

And this island's not bad; it's full of noises, sounds and
sweet airs, that give delight, and hurt not. So I can't
complain.

Uplifting music – modern.

And now the storm's gone, and Prospero's gone, I've
nothing or no one to fear apart from myself, and I'm a
monster, so it doesn't matter.

Music swells.

SHOPPING FOR SHOES

Shopping for Shoes was commissioned by Jenny Harris, Head of Education and Training for the National Theatre, and John Riches, Secondary Co-ordinator for the Art of Regeneration at the Albany, Deptford. It was first performed at St Ursula's School, Greenwich on 18 June 2003.

Thanks to Jenny Harris and John Riches at Art of Regeneration; Chris Lambert for stage management; Helen Prosser at the National; Kim Van Dooren; and Nike for providing some of the shoes without asking to read the story.

A simple platform, sloping towards the audience, chest-high and big enough to create a main 'acting' location plus space for a 'chorus'. Two poles rise up out of the back of the slope. Between these is strung a wire which will act as the telephone wire for the end of the story. Beneath the platform, accessible from behind, are shelves on which the shoes are arranged, invisible to the audience, ready to be used.

This platform is the stage around which the performer works and on which the shoes are manipulated. The shoes are never animated like conventional puppets, but each is given time, space and sometimes sound to assert itself.

It's traditional with these things to start 'Once upon a time'. But the time is now. It's happening now.

Siobhan McCluskey, Year Eight, is sitting wrapped in a damp towel: barefoot, red-faced and blotchy after a hot shower. Her dad is combing her hair for nits. Her older brother, Owen, is at work. She's sitting there – Channel Four News on the telly – occasionally, 'Ow, ow, don't kill them, Keith.' Her dad, Keith McCluskey, scrapes a tangled mass of hair and lice from the comb onto a piece of kitchen roll and studies his harvest. 'And big buggers too, Siobhan.' He will put them outside, ever so gently, on to a leaf. Keith McCluskey . . .

   Terrible sandals and jaunty whistling.

Elsewhere at this moment, Shaun Holmes, also Year Eight, 50 Cent on the stereo, is standing in front of a

mirror. It's not an ordinary mirror, but a special mirror
that his friend Quincy made for him. Quincy's in Year
Ten doing Design Technology. The mirror is like a
miniature dressing-table mirror, three-sided, but it sits on
the floor and it's no higher than a metre from top to
bottom. Shaun can't see his face in this mirror. What he
can see, though . . . Nike Vapour Supreme (*the shoes*).
Immaculate, spotless. Italian styling. Grey imports
bought by his Uncle Vince in New York and worth their
weight in gold. Literally. Shaun is transfixed by their
beauty. A triumph of style over function. A masterpiece.
A work of art. He presents his feet to the mirror,
searching for the perfect angle at which their brilliance
can be best expressed. Around Shaun, racked neatly in
rows, are maybe sixty pairs of shoes. Mostly the modern
Nike stuff: Air Jordan, Air Pegasus, Air Kukini, Air Max
Aggressor, Air Presto Velour, Vandalised Supreme, Shox
R4. But also the old collectors' stuff: Nike Cortez,
Wilsons, Jack Purcells, Corduroy Adidas, Adidas
Superstars, Gazelle, Suede Pumas, Puma Clydes and
so on. As you'll gather, Shaun likes shoes.

Now, right now, it's Friday morning and, since the Marcus
Garvey City Technology College took on European
opening hours, Siobhan has had great difficulties getting
it together. She's running very late, but she's not rushing.

Horrid puppy slippers.

If you listen carefully you can hear her humming Norah
Jones' 'Come Away with Me', as she waits for her toast.

Humming, feet shuffling.

Recently, Siobhan had her braces removed – and,
although she'll never feel it or know it, she's fast
becoming the prettiest girl in the school.

More humming.

Her eyes are heavy; she stayed up late last night, surfing the internet, chatting on MSN, talking to a Native American teenager in Idaho, signing online petitions against US conglomerates. But that's not what's on her mind right now.

More humming.

Not many people know it, but there's a corner of Siobhan McCluskey's heart that isn't hers. He's become a bit of an obsession for her. She writes his name in her drafting book, next to the Greenpeace logo. But the tragedy is, the tragedy of it all is, that he only has eyes for himself and his feet and, as Siobhan McCluskey goes out the front door . . .

Jelly shoes.

Siobhan believes in vegetarian shoes. She's been in the area less than a year but she's already an organiser for the Woodcraft Folk. She believes that meat is murder, that Nestlé are baby-killers, that The Gap runs sweatshops, that McDonalds have destroyed the rainforest, that Bush is worse than Hitler and that Blair is a poodle.

Shaun, on the other hand, believes in shoes and self-expression. And, by and large, he's allowed to express himself pretty well. His dad drives his own black cab . . .

Wide, Gucci loafers.

His dad loves shoes too; that's where Shaun gets it from. Ralph Lauren, Giorgio Armani, Gucci. He has a Christian Dior raincoat which he ostentatiously leaves on the back ledge of the cab. Business is good. They're planning to move out of the flats any time now. They're thinking Bexleyheath. Between his dad and Uncle Vince, Shaun is pretty much fixed whenever he wants to expand his collection. His mum works three nights a week in a casino.

White, four-inch stilettos.

Last night she got home at 2 a.m. Shaun has 130 channels on the TV in his bedroom, but he's never had a girlfriend; not a proper one. When he's older he's going to live in Florida. It's Friday morning and Shaun is left to look after two-year-old Letitia –

Baby shoes.

– who wakes at 6.30 and is put in front of Cbeebies with a bottle of juice and some biscuits. 'Shau, *Tellytubbies*, Shau, big hug, Shau.'

Siobhan's mother had what Keith described as 'a nervous collapse' in 1997 and now lives in a commune in Scotland.

Totally weird Scottish hippy-pixie shoes.

Siobhan travels up to Scotland on her own each summer to stay with her mum and her mum's German partner, Gunther.

German shoes in relation to the pixie shoes.

'Ya, Shiworn, a big hug for your Uncle Gunther.' Now, however, she is seriously late for school and will have to take the bus instead of walk. Owen, who works at night, is still in bed and will be till midday. Her dad Keith left the house at 7.00 for work at the cycling charity where he's campaigns co-ordinator. Keith is a big cyclist and left wearing skin-tight leggings with a padded crotch and matching fluorescent tabard and helmet.

Bizarre cycling shoes.

'Bye, darling.' 'Bye, Dad.' Siobhan is now taking the lift which smells of pee and has the word 'TWAT' painted across the door. She's dawdling towards the bus stop, humming and thinking about Shaun.

Jelly shoes travelling slowly.

Letitia settled, Shaun's going back to his room, where he begins his grooming. He's only just thirteen, but he thinks he's old enough to shave and he's training his bumfluff into a Craig David formation. Uncle Vince brought him back some fancy wax from LA which he works into his hair. And then the indecision begins as he casts his expert eye over his collection. Shaun is catholic in his taste; this means he's not totally exclusive to one particular brand. He would argue, though, that walking through the city streets with the famous Nike Swoosh on his sneakers is the poetry of resistance against the dull routine of the modern world. Shaun is a poet of the shoe. The Nike Swoosh, he says, is movement as mythology. After fifteen minutes of indecision he goes for his Nike Shox iDs – the ultimate expression of individuality – made at the factory with his own name stitched into the side.

Nike Shox iD.

He's standing before his special mirror and he feels complete. His mum has surfaced, wearing nothing but a far too revealing T-shirt.

Slippers.

Mum You're late.

Shaun I'm going.

Mum What do you say?

Shaun No, Mum.

Mum Come here.

Shaun No.

Mum Come here, my little man.

Shaun Mum. No–o–o–o.

And she chases him through the front door, traps him, kisses him and makes him tell her that he loves her. 'Love you.' Her breath smells of stale sleep. Shaun puts on his Walkman and takes the lift which smells of pee and has the word 'TWAT' painted across the door. Halfway to the bus stop he overtakes Siobhan –

Jelly shoes.

– who has just been passed over by the shadow of a plane heading for Heathrow and who's thinking how that must be good luck.

When Siobhan lowers her eyes she catches sight of the words 'Shaun Holmes' stitched onto a pair of trainers. In those shoes are the feet of the person who owns a little bit of her heart, and her pace (and her heart) quickens. Shaun and Siobhan arrive at the bus stop almost at the same time. They stand, almost within touching distance, in a queue of two old ladies and a couple of Year Sevens from Marcus Garvey who just snog all the time.

Two pairs of old-lady shoes plus two pairs of shoes from the audience form the chorus. Time is taken to map out this scene.

Siobhan McClusky knows every angle of Shaun's face, every contour of his clothed body. She's studied him in PE. Shaun Holmes, however, would be hard pushed to remember Siobhan's name, even though they're in the same set for Maths. Siobhan is a new girl; she's only been at the school a year. Unless you moved in her circles you'd not have had the time to really notice her. Siobhan is trying to attract Shaun's attention.

Two shoes perform a strange negotiation of space.

Eventually:

Siobhan Cool shoes.

Shaun looks over to her.

Shaun Uh?

He takes one earpiece out of his ear.

Siobhan Your coos are shool I mean your shoes are cool.

Shaun looks her up and down, down to her feet, down to her shoes, and then he offers her the most damning word ever given in the field of human communication.

Shaun Whatever.

He replaces the earpiece and looks up the road. This throws Siobhan and a lump appears in her throat. And then she really puts her foot in it.

Siobhan You're Shaun Holmes, aren't you?

Shaun What?

Siobhan I'm Siobhan McCluskey I'm in your maths set you live in Princes Court don't you so do I.

Silence.

Siobhan Some bloke once wrote and asked to have the word 'Sweatshop' put on a pair of them. They wrote back saying that you couldn't have a rude word. He said 'Sweatshop' wasn't rude. And they still said no.

And Siobhan gives a laugh, a laugh which is meant to sound like an all-embracing, right-on, feminine tinkle, but comes out sounding like a warthog choking on its breakfast. Siobhan turns red. Shaun turns away.

But as he turns away his left shoe comes slam into contact with the shoe's mortal enemy.

   A plastic dog turd.

Not a normal sized one, oh no, but a Great Dane–Rottweiler cross left by a Great Dane–Rottweiler cross –

   Another dog turd.

– who's just had colonic irrigation.

Another dog turd.

'Oooo dear,' says one old lady. 'Ooooo,' goes the other old lady. 'Mmmmmm,' go the two Year Sevens.

'Aaargh,' goes Shaun, and he lets out a scream which belies the fact he thinks his voice has broken. Hot tears prick his eyes as he looks down on where his shoe has landed firmly and fairly in the middle of the muck.

For Shaun, it is the end of the world. ('They're ruined, man, ruined.') For Siobhan, it is the beginning of HOPE.

Shaun Look what you made me do.

Siobhan I never . . .

Siobhan offers to get a stick to wipe it off, but there's more stuff here than you can shake a stick at. It's smeared up, obscuring part of his machine-stitched name. There's no way Shaun can go to school with these. He heads back home, Siobhan following him, apologising.

A long, negotiated journey.

Shaun Look, just piss off will you.

*

Early that evening there's a knock on Shaun's front door. Shaun opens it.

Nike flip-flops.

It's Siobhan –

Sensible vegetarian lace-ups personalised with colourful beads and symbols.

– looking rather lovely and carrying these.

68

A ghastly pair of secondhand men's trainers.

Siobhan Um, I'm sorry about this morning. I've brought these. They're my dad's. He never wears them. I reckon you're the same size. Nine? These are nine. You can have them. Just until you've cleaned up the others, if you like. Or you can keep them.

And, oddly, a little bit of ice melts inside Shaun's heart and he feels like a kindly teacher realising that there is work to be done, and he notices Siobhan's almond eyes and his pulse begins to beat a little faster. But, despite these feelings, he says:

Shaun You ain't got a clue, have you?

But Shaun invites Siobhan in. Into the flat in Princes Court. They pass through the lounge, where Letitia is asleep on the sofa –

Baby shoes.

– and Shaun's mum is sprawled in an armchair, smoking a cigarette.

Shiny boots, splayed out.

She's about to go to work. 'Bloody 'ell, Shaun. Who's your girlfriend?' And although a bit of Shaun wishes his mum would shut up, there's another bit which feels a warm glow of pride at the conjunction of his own name with the word 'girl' and the word 'friend'.

The pair go into Shaun's bedroom, where Siobhan is stunned by the sight that greets her. It's as though she's walked into a shoe shop. Shaun has scrubbed clean the Nike iDs, blow-dried them and replaced them at the centre of his collection. Sixty pairs of shoes leave little space for anything else. On the wall of his bedroom, in huge print, are the words 'JUST DO IT' and a giant Nike 'tick'. The two of them sit side by side on his bed. Shaun

69

puts on P Diddy. Their legs almost touch. Siobhan feels ridiculous with the scruffy pair of Primark's best she holds in her hand. Shaun sees Siobhan's look and, crucially, he mistakes it for envy.

Shaun Not bad, eh?

And Shaun tells her about his shoes. About belonging to a tribe, about being an individual, about feeling special, about being cool. The mythology of movement. About how these shoes are 'buff', these shoes are 'tick'. About how every shoe in his collection expresses a different bit of him. Every brand says something. *Just Do It.* Just do it. It means we can have what we want whenever we want it. He says he's got the same shoes as Justin Timberlake, Nelly, Eminem, you name it. He's got over £4,000 worth of shoes in here. People have been mugged for some of these shoes. It's about your identity. It's about who you are. 'I mean look at you; look at your shoes. Don't you realise how sad they are, how when people see you in them they think you're a minger. You should give it a bit more thought, Siobhan. You're a good-looking girl.'

And Siobhan sits there, silenced. With every word Shaun utters he seems to get smaller in her eyes. But he also looks so cute as he waves his arms around. And she should hate him but she finds she doesn't and she's confused that she doesn't. Part of her wants to stand up and slap Shaun Holmes. Part of her wants to pull him to her and kiss him till he bloody shuts up.

But then she has an idea. She flutters her eyelashes, and pulls her skirt tight down against her bum.

Siobhan I really like you, Shaun.

She says that a group of her friends are going bowling tonight, and did he want to come? Now, secretly, Shaun doesn't get asked out much. Certainly not by girls. He *goes* out, he *hangs* out, but he doesn't get *asked* out. And he's flattered. A bit of him thinks it would help Siobhan's image if she was seen with him.

Shaun Alright.

Siobhan You're not going in them, are you?

And Shaun turns to his collection. This calls for something special, something extraordinary, something head-turning. The jewel of his collection: the Nike Air Jordan Mark One. Huge, ankle-hugging, retro but with a timeless elegance and an immortal cool.

   The shoes.

Found through a specialist magazine. A little tight now, but worth the pain. Shaun slips on the shoes, his mum gives him a fiver and the two of them head out into the summer evening.

*

But there's something Shaun's forgotten about ten-pin bowling. Something absolutely fundamental to the experience. Something very much at the forefront of Siobhan's mind.

   Horrible bowling shoes.

Shaun I ain't putting them on.

Siobhan You have to or you can't play.

Shaun Who makes 'em?

Siobhan What?

Shaun Who makes 'em?

And so, excruciatingly, Shaun hands over his Nike Air Jordans to the spotty kid at the counter. Siobhan stifles her laughter as she winks at the spotty kid and watches Shaun wrestle with the laces of his ego as he puts on the bowling shoes. They go down to Lane 14, where there's Orlagh, Pria and Ayisha.

> *Five pairs of bowling shoes, Shaun's shoes sticking out like a sore thumb.*

Shaun is now desperately wishing he hadn't come and even more desperately hoping that none of his friends will see him. Not only is he wearing the geekiest shoes imaginable, he's surrounded by half the members of the School Council, the girls who organised the boycott of the Nestlé vending machine, who led the walk-out over the war in Iraq. He says very little and spends most of his time staring at Siobhan, which is his way of chatting someone up. They play one game. The girls are crap and spend most of their time giggling. Even though he hasn't played for years, Shaun wipes the board with them, which helps to repair his damaged ego.

They go up to the counter and Shaun cringes as the girls reclaim their nerdy shoes. It's his turn to retrieve his Nikes and feel human again. But the spotty kid comes back empty-handed. Shaun's shoes have gone, he says, and he smiles at Siobhan. Shaun feels like someone has punched him in the stomach. The girls are at the doors.

Siobhan Come on.

Shaun Wait. My shoes. My shoes are –

He looks to Siobhan, who has a huge grin on her face. The spotty kid at the counter is her brother, Owen, and in her hand she holds a pair of Nike Air Jordans Mark One.

Siobhan Come and get them.

Shaun is in his socks. Siobhan breaks from the gang; she goes through the door and out into the night. Shaun goes after her. Siobhan runs, Shaun chases. Siobhan laughs and, weirdly, Shaun finds himself wanting to laugh too. They pass the mall, out past McDonalds, KFC, TGI Fridays and up towards the railway bridge. Shaun has never been without shoes; his feet are tender and he finds it hard to run. He treads on loose chippings from the road; he hobbles on until he comes to a sudden stop on the bridge. There, lit by the sodium glare of a street light, standing on the bridge parapet, dangling the ultimate icons of cool above the busy mainline to Kent, is Siobhan, a glint in her eyes.

Shaun Don't do it.

Siobhan *Don't* do it? I thought I could '*Just* do it.'

Shaun Please, Siobhan. You'll fall. Come down.

Siobhan You said, with these, I could have what I wanted, when I wanted it. Just Do It, remember.

Shaun Shut up. Bloody shut up, Siobhan. People will see. Give 'em back. It's not funny.

Siobhan No, it's not bloody funny. Shall I tell you about your precious shoes, Shaun Holmes? Shall I Just Do It? Your shoes were probably made by some kid like you or me. Some scrawny kid working in a shit factory for shit hours for one quid a week so that you can feel a bit cool.

You ain't got a clue, have you?

Keith McCluskey would be so proud of his daughter. Shaun, meanwhile, is a little mesmerised by what's going on. He's confused that he's not feeling as angry as he thinks he should be. In fact, he's quite enjoying the experience, in his socks, in the night, watching a mad beautiful girl with fire in her eyes. And Siobhan goes on.

Siobhan And we're the mugs who go along with it. We think we're being so bloody individual by wearing the same stuff as everyone else, but we're just sheep. We're bloody sheep.

And with that, Siobhan hurls the Nike Air Jordans into the night sky.

Shaun (*slow motion sound*) Noooooooo . . .

The laces have been tied together and the shoes spin up into the orange glare.

Shoes spinning.

Stretched above the road there is a telephone wire. The shoes describe a perfect arc, twisting and spiralling. For a second there's a chance that they'll miss the wire, but then the left foot catches and the right just spins around it until they're well and truly tangled.

The Air Jordans hang from the wire above the platform.

And they hang there, like countless other trainers caught on countless other telephone wires. And Siobhan goes, 'Sheep.'

And Shaun is silent. His head and his heart fighting each other to the death.

He can't think of anything to say.

And then Shaun goes, 'Baaaaaaaa.'

The things he loved most in the world are dangling beyond his reach, but he doesn't seem to care any more. He's found something else to be interested in, and she's standing two feet away from him, panting, smiling, waiting for a response. And he doesn't know what to say. So, again, he goes, 'Baaaaaaa.'

And Siobhan looks at him and then she goes, 'Baaaaaaaa.' And the two of them begin to laugh, and the two of them

74

bleat like sheep. And then Siobhan reaches down, slips off her own shoes, ties the laces together and throws them high out up to the telephone wire –

Shoes spinning.

– where they catch, and where they dangle to this day, side by side with a pair of collectors' Nike Air Jordans Mark One.

Siobhan's shoes also hang from the wire.

Siobhan puts out her hand. Shaun takes it and he helps her down from the wall. They stand and face each other, searching each other's eyes for some understanding of what has happened.

Siobhan Sorry about your shoes.

Shaun It's OK. I've got plenty.

Neither knows what it means. But they smile at each other. An uncertain smile. And they walk back to Princes Court.

Barefoot.